Living and Non-living in the Ocean

Rebecca Rissman

Raintree is an imprint of Capstone Global Library Limited, a company incorporated in England and Wales having its registered office at 7 Pilgrim Street, London, EC4V 6LB – Registered company number: 6695582

To contact Raintree:
Phone: 0845 6044371
Fax: + 44 (0) 1865 312263
Email: myorders@raintreepublishers.co.uk
Outside the UK please telephone +44 1865 312262.

Text © Capstone Global Library Limited 2014
First published in hardback in 2014
The moral rights of the proprietor have been asserted.

Edited by Daniel Nunn, Rebecca Rissman, and Catherine Veitch
Designed by Cynthia Della-Rovere
Picture research by Tracy Cummins
Production by Sophia Argyris
Originated by Capstone Global Library Ltd
Printed and bound in China by Leo Paper Products Ltd

ISBN 978 1 406 26589 7
17 16 15 14 13
10 9 8 7 6 5 4 3 2 1

British Library Cataloguing in Publication Data
A full catalogue record for this book is available from the British Library.

Acknowledgements
We would like to thank the following for permission to reproduce photographs: Getty Images pp. 15 (Visuals Unlimited), 18 (Nature/UIG), 20 (Steven Trainoff Ph.D.); istockphoto p. 9 (© microgen); Photo Researchers p. 10 (Andrew J. Martinez); Shutterstock pp. 1 (© trekandshoot), 4 (© Alberto Pérez Veiga), 5 (© Rich Carey), 6, 23a (© cbpix), 7 (© Rich Carey), 8 (© A Cotton Photo), 12 (© Pichugin Dmitry), 13 (© whitewizzard), 14 (© Levent Konuk), 16 (© Anna segeren), 17, 23c (© designsstock), 19 (© Ekaterina Lin), 21 (© worldswildlifewonders), 22 (© Volodymyr Goinyk), 23d (© Galyna Andrushko); Superstock p. 11, 23b (© age fotostock).

Front cover photograph of a coral reef in Bali, Indonesia reproduced with permission of Superstock (© Tips Images).

We would like to thank Michael Bright and Diana Bentley for their invaluable help in the preparation of this book.

Every effort has been made to contact copyright holders of material reproduced in this book. Any omissions will be rectified in subsequent printings if notice is given to the publisher.

All the Internet addresses (URLs) given in this book were valid at the time of going to press. However, due to the dynamic nature of the Internet, some addresses may have changed, or sites may have changed or ceased to exist since publication. While the author and publisher regret any inconvenience this may cause readers, no responsibility for any such changes can be accepted by either the author or the publisher.

Some words are in bold, **like this**.
You can find them in the glossary on page 23.

Contents

What is an ocean?

An ocean is a very large body of water.

Oceans are full of salt water.

Different types of plants and animals live in the oceans.

There are **non-living** things in the oceans, too.

What are living things?

Living things are alive. Living things need air and **sunlight**. Living things move on their own.

Living things need food and water.

Living things grow and change.

What are non-living things?

Non-living things are not alive. Non-living things do not need air and **sunlight**.

Non-living things do not need food or water.

Non-living things do not move on their own.

Non-living things do not grow and change on their own.

Is a lobster living or non-living?

A **lobster** needs food and water.

A lobster moves on its own.

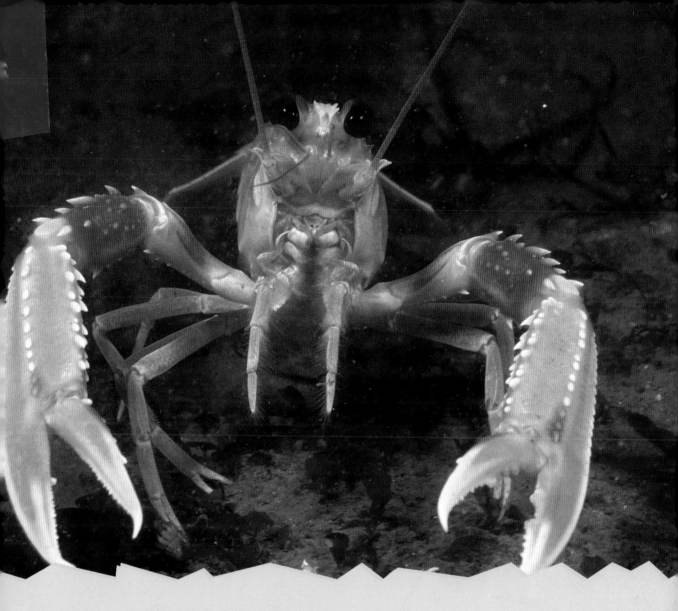

A lobster grows and changes.

A lobster needs air and **sunlight**.

A lobster is **living**.

Is a rock living or non-living?

A rock does not need food or water.

A rock does not move on its own.

A rock does not grow and change on its own.

A rock does not need air or **sunlight**.

A rock is **non-living**.

Is a fish living or non-living?

A fish grows and changes.

A fish needs food and water.

A fish moves on its own.

A fish needs air and **sunlight**.

A fish is **living**.

Is sand living or non-living?

Sand does not move on its own.

Sand does not need food or water.

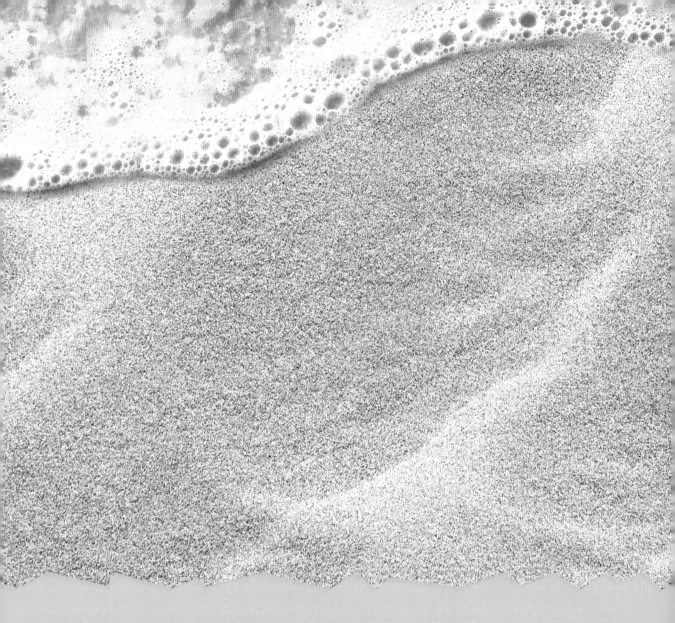

Sand does not grow on its own.

Sand does not need air or **sunlight**.

Sand is **non-living**.

Is a dolphin living or non-living?

A dolphin grows and changes.

A dolphin needs food and water.

A dolphin moves on its own.

A dolphin needs air and **sunlight**.

A dolphin is **living**.

Is seaweed living or non-living?

Seaweed moves on its own towards the sun.

Seaweed gets food from the sun.

Seaweed grows and changes.

Seaweed needs air and **sunlight**.

Seaweed is **living**.

What do you think?

Is this iceberg **living** or **non-living**?

Glossary

living alive. Living things need food and water. They breathe and move on their own. They grow and change.

lobster animal that lives in the ocean. It has a hard shell and big claws.

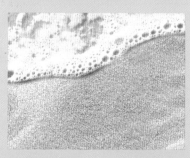

non-living not alive. Non-living things do not need food and water. They do not move on their own. They do not grow and change on their own.

sunlight light from the sun

Find out more

Websites
Click through these images of living and non-living things, then take a quiz!
www.bbc.co.uk/schools/scienceclips/ages/5_6/ourselves.shtml

Check out this site to learn more about what living things need.
www.kidsbiology.com/biology_basics/needs_living_things/living_things_have_needs1.php

Go to this site and try to spot all the living things in the park!
www.sciencekids.co.nz/gamesactivities/plantsanimals.html

Books
About Habitats: Oceans, Cathryn Sill (Peachtree Publishers, 2009)

Living and Nonliving, Carol K. Lindeen (Capstone Press, 2008)

Ocean of Animals (Habitats Around the World), Janine Scott (Capstone Press, 2011)

Index